Academic Writing
AI Prompts Phrasebook

ACADEMIC WRITING AI PROMPTS PHRASEBOOK

DR BRON EAGER

*For all the writers and
researchers making their way
through this thrilling and terrifying
world of AI in Higher Ed.*

Welcome

I'm delighted to have you as a reader and excited to share with you over 500 prompts to help accelerate your academic writing and research. With these prompts, you'll never again be stuck staring at a blank page.

Whether you're a seasoned academic or just starting out, these prompts are designed to help you refine your skills to thrive in a new world of academic work powered by Artificial Intelligence.

I can't wait to see what you create!

Explore

Introduction

What are prompts?

Prompts are short phrases or sentences that are inputted by the user to initiate a conversation or request a response from the AI language model.

Prompts can be used to initiate a wide variety of conversations or tasks, ranging from generating ideas for a writing project to seeking help with improving sentence structure or formatting tables and figures.

When a prompt is inputted into ChatGPT, the language model analyzes the input and generates a response based on its vast knowledge base and understanding of natural language. This response may include suggestions, feedback, or ideas to help the user with their specific request or task.

For researchers in particular, prompts can be an invaluable tool for improving their academic writing skills.

By inputting a prompt related to a specific area of writing that they need assistance with, such as generating ideas or refining arguments, researchers can receive customized feedback and guidance from ChatGPT to help them achieve their writing goals.

Overall, prompts in ChatGPT offer a powerful tool for enhancing communication and productivity, providing users with tailored responses and support for a wide range of tasks and needs.

How to use prompts

Using prompts with ChatGPT is a simple and effective way to improve your academic writing skills. In this section, I provide a step-by-step guide on how to use prompts with ChatGPT to enhance your research and writing.

Step 1: Identify your specific writing needs

The first step in using prompts with ChatGPT is to identify your specific writing needs. Consider what areas of your research or writing could benefit from additional support or guidance. Do you need help generating ideas? Are you struggling with sentence structure? Do you need to improve your arguments or incorporate primary sources more effectively? Once you have identified your specific needs, you can begin to formulate prompts to input into ChatGPT.

Step 2: Formulate your prompts

The second step is to formulate your prompts. Prompts can be as simple or as detailed as you like, depending on your specific needs. For example, if you're struggling to generate ideas for a new research project, you might input a prompt such as "What are some potential research questions related to [insert research topic]?" Alternatively, if you need help refining your arguments, you might input a prompt such as "How can I strengthen my argument that [insert thesis statement]?"

Luckily, because you're reading this book, you've got over 500 prompts already crafted for you to help you achieve your writing and research tasks.

Step 3: Input your prompts into ChatGPT

The third step is to input your prompts into ChatGPT. To do this, simply navigate to the ChatGPT website, or interface of your choice, and enter your prompt into the chat box. ChatGPT will then analyze your input and generate a response.

Step 4: Review and incorporate ChatGPT's response

The fourth step is to review and incorporate ChatGPT's response. ChatGPT's response may include suggestions, feedback, or ideas to help you with your specific request or task. Take the time to carefully review and consider these suggestions, and incorporate them into your writing as needed. Remember that the ultimate goal is to improve the quality of your writing and research, so be open to incorporating new ideas and approaches as you go. Also, it's good to know that ChatGPT has a tendency to 'make things up', so always ensure that any facts mentioned in the generated output are correct before using them in your work.

Step 5: Repeat the process as needed

The final step is to repeat the process as needed. Depending on the scope and complexity of your writing project, you may need to input multiple prompts into ChatGPT over time. Don't be afraid to experiment with different prompts and approaches to see what works best for you. With time and practice, you'll become more comfortable using prompts with ChatGPT and more adept at improving your writing and research skills.

Have fun!

Notes

You'll find *Notes* pages throughout the book. Use them to record your own prompts and learnings.

The prompts in this book are crafted to be used with ChatGPT, an AI language model that you can access at
https://chat.openai.com

The prompts are versatile and can be used with any AI language model to explore the exciting world of academic writing and research using Artificial Intelligence.

Prompts

The following pages contain a wealth of prompts designed to help accelerate your academic writing and research.

These prompts are specifically crafted to help you overcome common writing challenges, refine your research and writing skills, and produce high-quality work that is both engaging and impactful.

Generating topic ideas for research papers

- "What are some current gaps or limitations in [research area] that could benefit from a novel research approach?"
- "How can [specific technology or methodology] be applied in [research area] to answer unanswered questions or shed new light on existing knowledge?"
- "What are the key factors driving [trend or issue] in [research area], and how can researchers address these factors to advance the field?"
- "What are the ethical considerations that researchers should take into account when studying [topic or issue], and how can these considerations be addressed in a research project?"
- "How can insights from [related field] be integrated into [research area] to generate new hypotheses or directions for research?"
- "What are some of the challenges facing [target population or group] in relation to [issue or problem], and how can research help address these challenges?"
- "What are some of the potential implications of [recent development or discovery] in [research area], and how can researchers explore these implications in a research project?"
- "How can researchers use data from [specific source] to gain new insights into [research area], and what are some potential limitations or challenges in using this data?"

Generating topic ideas for research papers

- "What are the key factors driving [method or approach] in [research area], and how can researchers evaluate the effectiveness of this method or approach in a research project?"
- "How can researchers use [specific tool or resource] to facilitate [research goal or objective] in [research area], and what are some potential applications of this tool or resource in future research projects?"
- "What are some of the key theoretical frameworks or concepts that have been used to understand [research area], and how can researchers use these frameworks to generate new research questions or directions?"
- "How can researchers collaborate with [industry, government, community groups, etc.] to ensure that their research addresses real-world challenges and has practical applications?"
- "What are some of the ethical considerations that arise when conducting research with [specific population or group], and how can these considerations be addressed in a research project?"
- "How can researchers use data visualization techniques to communicate complex findings or relationships in [research area], and what are some potential applications of these techniques?"
- "What are some of the current debates or controversies in [research area], and how can researchers contribute to these discussions through their research?"
- "How can researchers use interdisciplinary approaches to generate new insights or approaches in [research area], and what are some potential challenges or limitations of interdisciplinary research?"

Generating topic ideas for research papers

- "What are some of the historical trends or patterns in [research area], and how can researchers use this historical perspective to inform their current research questions or hypotheses?"
- "What are some of the potential biases or limitations in [specific methodology or approach] in [research area], and how can researchers address these issues in their research?"
- "How can researchers use machine learning or artificial intelligence techniques to analyze large datasets in [research area], and what are some potential applications of these techniques?"
- "How can researchers design studies that take into account individual differences in [specific trait or characteristic] in [research area], and what are some potential implications of these individual differences for research findings or applications?"

Research proposals

- "Can you provide some suggestions on how to structure my research proposal in [research area or topic] to effectively communicate the research question or problem, methodology, and expected outcomes?"
- "I'm struggling to identify the most relevant and significant research questions or problems to address in my research proposal in [research area or topic]. Can you provide some guidance on how to approach this?"
- "What strategies can I use to effectively use the literature review to justify the significance and relevance of my research proposal in [research area or topic]?"
- "Can you suggest some ways to use the theoretical framework to effectively guide and inform the research design and methods in my research proposal in [research area or topic]?"
- "I need help identifying the appropriate research design and methods to use in my research proposal in [research area or topic]. Can you provide some guidance on how to approach this?"
- "How can I effectively use visual aids and multimedia tools to communicate the research objectives and methodology in my research proposal in [research area or topic]?"
- "Can you provide some suggestions on how to use persuasive language and rhetoric to effectively appeal to the significance and relevance of my research proposal in [research area or topic]?"

- "I'm struggling to effectively use the research question or problem to guide the development and execution of the research project in my research proposal in [research area or topic]. Can you provide some guidance on how to approach this?"
- "What strategies can I use to effectively anticipate and address potential limitations and challenges in my research proposal in [research area or topic]?"
- "Can you suggest some ways to use the research findings and outcomes to effectively inform and influence policy and practice in my research area or topic?"
- "I need help identifying the appropriate sample size and sampling methods to use in my research proposal in [research area or topic]. Can you provide some guidance on how to approach this?"
- "How can I effectively use the research methodology to ensure the reliability and validity of the research findings in my research proposal in [research area or topic]?"
- "Can you provide some suggestions on how to use the expected outcomes to effectively demonstrate the potential impact and contributions of my research proposal in [research area or topic]?"
- "I'm struggling to effectively use the research hypothesis to guide the development and execution of the research project in my research proposal in [research area or topic]. Can you provide some guidance on how to approach this?"

Research proposals

- "What strategies can I use to effectively use the research objectives to guide the development and execution of the research project in my research proposal in [research area or topic]?"
- "Can you suggest some ways to use the research methods to effectively capture and analyze the relevant data and evidence in my research proposal in [research area or topic]?"
- "I need help identifying the appropriate data analysis methods to use in my research proposal in [research area or topic]. Can you provide some guidance on how to approach this?"
- "How can I effectively use the research project timeline to ensure the feasibility and efficiency of the research project in my research proposal in [research area or topic]?"
- "Can you provide some suggestions on how to use the research funding and resources to effectively support the development and execution of the research project in my research proposal in [research area or topic]?"
- "I'm struggling to effectively use the research literature to inform and support the development of the research proposal in [research area or topic]. Can you provide some guidance on how to approach this?"

Thesis statement development

- "Can you help me develop a clear and concise thesis statement for my research on [research area or topic]?"
- "I'm having trouble refining my thesis statement for my paper on [area of interest]. Can you provide some suggestions?"
- "I need help developing a thesis statement that effectively captures the main argument of my research on [research area or topic]."
- "Can you provide some guidance on how to develop a strong and compelling thesis statement for my research on [research area or topic]?"
- "I'm struggling to come up with a clear thesis statement for my paper on [area of interest]. Can you help me brainstorm some ideas?"
- "How can I refine my thesis statement for my research on [research area or topic] to make it more specific and focused?"
- "Can you suggest some strategies for developing a thesis statement that effectively communicates the main argument of my research on [research area or topic]?"
- "I'm having trouble identifying the central argument of my research on [research area or topic]. Can you help me develop a thesis statement that captures it?"
- "How can I develop a thesis statement that effectively addresses the main research question of my study on [research area or topic]?"

Thesis statement development

- "Can you provide some examples of effective thesis statements for research on [research area or topic] to help me refine my own statement?"
- "I need help developing a thesis statement that takes into account the various perspectives and arguments related to my research on [research area or topic]."
- "Can you help me develop a thesis statement that clearly articulates the significance and contribution of my research on [research area or topic]?"
- "What strategies can I use to develop a thesis statement that effectively captures the main findings of my research on [research area or topic]?"
- "I'm struggling to develop a thesis statement that effectively communicates the scope and objectives of my research on [research area or topic]. Can you help me refine it?"
- "Can you provide some guidance on how to develop a thesis statement that effectively addresses the gaps or limitations in existing research on [research area or topic]?"
- "I'm having trouble developing a thesis statement that effectively addresses the research problem or hypothesis of my study on [research area or topic]. Can you provide some suggestions?"
- "What strategies can I use to develop a thesis statement that effectively addresses the research questions and objectives of my study on [research area or topic]?"

Thesis statement development

- "Can you help me develop a thesis statement that effectively communicates the methodology and approach of my research on [research area or topic]?"
- "How can I develop a thesis statement that effectively communicates the theoretical framework or conceptual framework of my research on [research area or topic]?"
- "I need help developing a thesis statement that effectively communicates the practical or policy implications of my research on [research area or topic]. Can you provide some suggestions?"

Gaps in the literature

- "What are the most pressing unanswered questions in [research area], and how can researchers design studies to address these questions?"
- "What are the current limitations or gaps in our knowledge of [specific topic or phenomenon] in [research area], and how can researchers design studies to fill these gaps?"
- "How can researchers identify gaps in the literature on [specific aspect or feature] in [research area], and what are some potential research questions or hypotheses that could address these gaps?"
- "What are the most recent developments or advances in [research area], and how can researchers determine whether there are still gaps in our understanding of these developments or areas for further investigation?"
- "What are the key challenges or obstacles facing researchers in [research area], and how can researchers design studies that specifically address these challenges or obstacles?"
- "What are some of the key assumptions or biases that may be limiting our understanding of [specific topic or phenomenon] in [research area], and how can researchers design studies to overcome these limitations?"
- "How can researchers use meta-analysis or systematic review techniques to identify gaps in the literature on [specific topic or phenomenon] in [research area], and what are some potential research questions or hypotheses that could address these gaps?"

- "What are the most commonly studied aspects or features of [research area], and how can researchers identify gaps in the literature on less-studied or under-studied aspects or features?"
- "What are some of the key unanswered questions or areas of disagreement among researchers in [research area], and how can researchers design studies that address these questions or areas of disagreement?"
- "What are the most common research methods or approaches used in [research area], and how can researchers design studies that use alternative or complementary methods or approaches to address gaps in the literature?"
- "What are some of the most recent trends or developments in [research area], and how can researchers determine whether these trends or developments are being adequately addressed in the literature?"
- "What are the most common variables or factors studied in relation to [specific topic or phenomenon] in [research area], and how can researchers identify gaps in the literature on less-studied or under-studied variables or factors?"
- "What are some of the most significant challenges facing practitioners or policymakers in [related field], and how can researchers identify gaps in the literature on research that can address these challenges?"
- "What are some of the potential ethical or legal implications of research in [research area], and how can researchers identify gaps in the literature on research that can address these implications?"

Gaps in the literature

- "What are some of the most common research designs used in [research area], and how can researchers design studies that use alternative or novel research designs to address gaps in the literature?"
- "What are the most common outcomes or measures used in studies of [specific topic or phenomenon] in [research area], and how can researchers identify gaps in the literature on less commonly used or novel outcomes or measures?"
- "What are the most commonly studied populations or samples in [research area], and how can researchers identify gaps in the literature on less-studied or underrepresented populations or samples?"
- "What are some of the key theoretical or conceptual frameworks used in [research area], and how can researchers identify gaps in the literature on research that uses alternative or complementary frameworks?"
- "What are some of the potential implications or applications of research in [research area] for [specific area or industry], and how can researchers identify gaps in the literature on research that can address these implications or applications?"
- "What are some of the most significant controversies or debates in [research area], and how can researchers identify gaps in the literature on research that can contribute to these discussions or debates?"

Supporting arguments

- "Can you help me brainstorm some supporting arguments for my paper on [research area or topic]?"
- "I'm having trouble coming up with supporting evidence for my paper on [area of interest]. Can you provide some suggestions?"
- "How can I develop strong arguments to support the main thesis of my paper on [research area or topic]?"
- "Can you suggest some research studies or examples that can be used as supporting evidence for my paper on [research area or topic]?"
- "I need help identifying some key arguments to support my main thesis for my paper on [area of interest]. Can you help me brainstorm some ideas?"
- "What strategies can I use to develop strong and compelling arguments to support my main thesis for my paper on [research area or topic]?"
- "Can you provide some guidance on how to effectively incorporate supporting evidence into my paper on [research area or topic]?"
- "I'm struggling to come up with arguments that effectively address the counterarguments and alternative perspectives related to my research on [research area or topic]. Can you provide some suggestions?"
- "How can I develop a coherent and logical sequence of supporting arguments for my paper on [research area or topic]?"

- "Can you suggest some sources or experts that can be used to strengthen the supporting arguments for my paper on [research area or topic]?"
- "I need help identifying the most relevant and persuasive evidence to support the main thesis of my paper on [research area or topic]. Can you provide some guidance?"
- "What strategies can I use to develop supporting arguments that effectively address the research questions and objectives of my paper on [research area or topic]?"
- "Can you suggest some effective rhetorical strategies to use when presenting supporting evidence for my paper on [research area or topic]?"
- "I'm struggling to come up with arguments that effectively address the practical or policy implications of my research on [research area or topic]. Can you provide some suggestions?"
- "How can I develop supporting arguments that effectively communicate the theoretical framework or conceptual framework of my research on [research area or topic]?"
- "Can you help me identify some key data or statistics that can be used as supporting evidence for my paper on [research area or topic]?"
- "What strategies can I use to develop arguments that effectively address the limitations or gaps in existing research related to my paper on [research area or topic]?"

Supporting arguments

- "I'm having trouble developing arguments that effectively address the ethical or social implications of my research on [research area or topic]. Can you provide some suggestions?"
- "Can you help me identify some key trends or patterns in existing research that can be used to support the arguments in my paper on [research area or topic]?"
- "How can I develop supporting arguments that effectively communicate the historical or cultural context of my research on [research area or topic]?"

Subtopics for an outline

- "Can you help me generate some subtopics for my outline on [research area or topic]?"
- "I'm struggling to come up with subtopics for my outline on [area of interest]. Can you provide some suggestions?"
- "How can I effectively organize my paper on [research area or topic] by developing subtopics for my outline?"
- "Can you suggest some key themes or ideas that can be used as subtopics for my outline on [research area or topic]?"
- "I need help identifying some specific areas of focus to include as subtopics in my outline on [area of interest]. Can you help me brainstorm some ideas?"
- "What strategies can I use to develop subtopics that effectively address the research questions and objectives of my study on [research area or topic]?"
- "Can you provide some guidance on how to develop subtopics that effectively communicate the theoretical framework or conceptual framework of my research on [research area or topic]?"
- "I'm having trouble organizing my ideas into subtopics that effectively address the main thesis of my paper on [research area or topic]. Can you provide some suggestions?"
- "How can I effectively incorporate supporting evidence into my subtopics to strengthen the overall argument of my paper on [research area or topic]?"
- "Can you suggest some experts or sources that can be used to strengthen the subtopics of my outline on [research area or topic]?"

- "I need help identifying the most relevant and persuasive subtopics to support the main thesis of my paper on [research area or topic]. Can you provide some guidance?"
- "What strategies can I use to develop subtopics that effectively address the counterarguments and alternative perspectives related to my research on [research area or topic]?"
- "Can you suggest some effective rhetorical strategies to use when presenting subtopics in my outline on [research area or topic]?"
- "I'm struggling to come up with subtopics that effectively address the practical or policy implications of my research on [research area or topic]. Can you provide some suggestions?"
- "How can I develop subtopics that effectively address the limitations or gaps in existing research related to my paper on [research area or topic]?"
- "Can you help me identify some key data or statistics that can be used as subtopics in my outline on [research area or topic]?"
- "What strategies can I use to develop subtopics that effectively address the ethical or social implications of my research on [research area or topic]?"
- "I need help identifying the most significant historical or cultural themes to include as subtopics in my outline on [research area or topic]. Can you provide some guidance?"

Subtopics for an outline

- "Can you suggest some key subtopics related to the methodology or approach of my research on [research area or topic]?"
- "How can I effectively structure my subtopics to create a logical and coherent sequence of ideas in my outline on [research area or topic]?"

Keywords for literature searches

- "Can you suggest some keywords or phrases to use when searching for literature on [research area or topic]?"
- "I'm having trouble finding relevant literature for my research on [area of interest]. Can you provide some guidance on how to generate effective keywords for my search?"
- "How can I develop a list of keywords and synonyms that effectively capture the scope and focus of my research on [research area or topic]?"
- "Can you suggest some terms or phrases that are commonly used in the literature related to my research on [research area or topic]?"
- "I need help identifying some specific terms or phrases related to my research on [area of interest] that can be used as keywords for my literature search. Can you help me brainstorm some ideas?"
- "What strategies can I use to develop keywords that effectively address the research questions and objectives of my study on [research area or topic]?"
- "Can you provide some guidance on how to effectively use Boolean operators and other search techniques to refine my keywords and search results?"
- "I'm having trouble finding literature that effectively addresses the theoretical or conceptual framework of my research on [research area or topic]. Can you suggest some keywords to use in my search?"

Keywords for literature searches

- "How can I effectively use subject headings and other controlled vocabulary to generate keywords for my literature search on [research area or topic]?"
- "Can you suggest some key authors or experts in my research area that can be used as keywords for my literature search?"
- "I need help identifying the most relevant and specific keywords to use in my literature search on [research area or topic]. Can you provide some guidance?"
- "What strategies can I use to identify alternative terms and synonyms that can be used as keywords for my literature search on [research area or topic]?"
- "Can you suggest some databases or sources that are most relevant to my research on [research area or topic] and can help me generate effective keywords?"
- "I'm struggling to find literature that effectively addresses the practical or policy implications of my research on [research area or topic]. Can you suggest some keywords to use in my search?"
- "How can I use the citation lists of relevant articles and books to generate keywords for my literature search on [research area or topic]?"
- "Can you help me identify some key terms or phrases related to the methodology or approach of my research on [research area or topic] that can be used as keywords for my literature search?"
- "What strategies can I use to identify the most current and relevant keywords for my literature search on [research area or topic]?"

Keywords for literature searches

- "I need help generating keywords that effectively address the limitations or gaps in existing research related to my paper on [research area or topic]. Can you provide some suggestions?"
- "Can you suggest some effective keyword combinations or phrases to use when searching for literature on [research area or topic]?"
- "How can I effectively use the abstracts and subject headings of relevant articles and books to generate keywords for my literature search on [research area or topic]?"

Transitions between paragraphs

- "Can you help me rephrase the transition between [insert paragraph 1] and [insert paragraph 2] in my paper on [research area or topic] to create a more coherent and logical flow?"
- "I'm having trouble transitioning between two paragraphs in my paper on [area of interest]. Can you help me rephrase the text to create a more cohesive argument?"
- "How can I effectively use transition words and phrases to connect the ideas and arguments presented in [insert paragraph 1] and [insert paragraph 2] in my paper on [research area or topic]?"
- "Can you provide some guidance on how to develop a logical and coherent sequence of ideas between two paragraphs in my paper on [research area or topic]?"
- "I need help identifying the most effective and appropriate transition words and phrases to use between [insert paragraph 1] and [insert paragraph 2]. Can you provide some suggestions?"
- "What strategies can I use to ensure that the transition between two paragraphs in my paper on [research area or topic] effectively communicates the main argument and thesis of my study?"
- "Can you suggest some effective rhetorical strategies to use when transitioning between paragraphs in my paper on [research area or topic]?"

- "I'm struggling to transition between two paragraphs in my paper on [area of interest] in a way that effectively addresses the research questions and objectives. Can you provide some guidance?"
- "How can I effectively use the topic sentences of the two paragraphs to develop a more effective transition between them in my paper on [research area or topic]?"
- "Can you suggest some key terms or phrases related to my research on [research area or topic] that can be used to develop an effective transition between two paragraphs in my paper?"
- "I need help rephrasing the text between [insert paragraph 1] and [insert paragraph 2] to more effectively communicate the significance and contribution of my research on [research area or topic]. Can you provide some suggestions?"
- "What strategies can I use to effectively transition between two paragraphs in my paper on [research area or topic] without repeating information or becoming redundant?"
- "Can you suggest some effective ways to use evidence and supporting examples when transitioning between two paragraphs in my paper on [research area or topic]?"
- "I'm having trouble transitioning between two paragraphs in my paper on [area of interest] in a way that effectively addresses the limitations or gaps in existing research. Can you provide some guidance?"
- "How can I effectively use the conclusion of the first paragraph to develop a more effective transition to the second paragraph in my paper on [research area or topic]?"

Transitions between paragraphs

- "Can you suggest some effective ways to use language and tone when transitioning between two paragraphs in my paper on [research area or topic]?"
- "I need help identifying the most effective ways to use the logical sequence of ideas between two paragraphs to develop a more effective transition in my paper on [research area or topic]. Can you provide some guidance?"
- "What strategies can I use to develop an effective transition between two paragraphs in my paper on [research area or topic] that effectively addresses the research questions and objectives?"
- "Can you suggest some effective ways to use visual aids, such as charts or graphs, to transition between two paragraphs in my paper on [research area or topic]?"
- "How can I effectively use the tone and voice of my writing to develop a more effective transition between two paragraphs in my paper on [research area or topic]?"

Improving sentence structure and grammar

- "Can you suggest ways to improve the sentence structure and grammar in [insert writing sample here] to make it more clear and concise?"
- "I'm having trouble with the sentence structure and grammar in my paper on [research area or topic]. Can you provide some guidance on how to improve it?"
- "How can I effectively use punctuation and sentence structure to improve the clarity and coherence of my writing in [insert writing sample here]?"
- "Can you provide some suggestions on how to vary sentence length and structure in [insert writing sample here] to create a more engaging and readable text?"
- "I need help identifying and correcting grammar errors in [insert writing sample here]. Can you provide some guidance on common mistakes to avoid?"
- "What strategies can I use to improve the syntax and grammar in [insert writing sample here] without changing the meaning or intent of the text?"
- "Can you suggest some effective ways to use active voice and passive voice to improve the clarity and coherence of my writing in [insert writing sample here]?"
- "I'm struggling with sentence fragments and run-on sentences in my writing on [research area or topic]. Can you provide some guidance on how to fix these issues?"

Improving sentence structure and grammar

- "How can I effectively use transitions and conjunctions to improve the flow and coherence of my writing in [insert writing sample here]?"
- "Can you suggest some strategies to improve the use of verb tenses in [insert writing sample here] to accurately convey the timing and sequencing of events or ideas?"
- "I need help identifying and correcting common errors in subject-verb agreement in [insert writing sample here]. Can you provide some guidance?"
- "What strategies can I use to improve the use of prepositions and articles in [insert writing sample here] to make it more clear and concise?"
- "Can you suggest some ways to simplify complex sentences and phrases in [insert writing sample here] to make it more readable and accessible?"
- "I'm having trouble with word choice and sentence structure in my writing on [area of interest]. Can you provide some guidance on how to choose the right words and phrases to convey my meaning?"
- "How can I effectively use parallel structure and lists to improve the clarity and coherence of my writing in [insert writing sample here]?"
- "Can you provide some suggestions on how to use the active voice in [insert writing sample here] to create a more engaging and dynamic text?"
- "I need help identifying and correcting errors in punctuation, such as commas and semicolons, in [insert writing sample here]. Can you provide some guidance?"

Improving sentence structure and grammar

- "What strategies can I use to improve the use of modifiers and phrases in [insert writing sample here] to create a more precise and descriptive text?"
- "Can you suggest some effective ways to use sentence variety and structure to improve the readability and interest of my writing in [insert writing sample here]?"
- "How can I effectively use subject-verb-object structure and sentence length to improve the clarity and coherence of my writing in [insert writing sample here]?"

Incorporating primary sources into a paper

- "Can you suggest some ways to incorporate primary sources into [insert writing sample here] to strengthen my argument and support my claims?"
- "I'm having trouble integrating primary sources into my paper on [research area or topic]. Can you provide some guidance on how to effectively use them?"
- "How can I use primary sources to add depth and complexity to my analysis in [insert writing sample here]?"
- "Can you provide some suggestions on how to use primary sources to offer a unique perspective or interpretation of my research area or topic in [insert writing sample here]?"
- "I need help identifying the most relevant and valuable primary sources to use in my paper on [research area or topic]. Can you provide some guidance on how to find them?"
- "What strategies can I use to analyze and interpret primary sources in [insert writing sample here] to develop a more nuanced and sophisticated argument?"
- "Can you suggest some ways to incorporate primary sources into my writing in a way that supports my thesis and advances my argument in [insert writing sample here]?"
- "I'm struggling to use primary sources effectively in my paper on [area of interest]. Can you provide some guidance on how to avoid common pitfalls and mistakes?"

Incorporating primary sources into a paper

- "How can I use primary sources to provide evidence for my claims and ideas in [insert writing sample here]?"
- "Can you suggest some effective ways to use quotations and paraphrases from primary sources to support my argument in [insert writing sample here]?"
- "I need help identifying the most appropriate and useful primary sources to use in my paper on [research area or topic]. Can you provide some guidance on how to evaluate them?"
- "What strategies can I use to integrate primary sources into my paper on [research area or topic] in a way that adds depth and complexity to my argument?"
- "Can you suggest some ways to use primary sources to respond to and engage with the existing scholarship on my research area or topic in [insert writing sample here]?"
- "I'm having trouble finding primary sources related to my research area or topic. Can you provide some guidance on how to expand my search?"
- "How can I use primary sources to offer a new perspective or interpretation of my research area or topic in [insert writing sample here]?"
- "Can you suggest some effective ways to use primary sources to develop a more nuanced and sophisticated understanding of my research area or topic in [insert writing sample here]?"
- "I need help identifying the most appropriate and useful primary sources to use in my paper on [research area or topic]. Can you provide some guidance on how to organize them effectively?"

Incorporating primary sources into a paper

- "What strategies can I use to analyze and interpret primary sources in [insert writing sample here] to develop a more nuanced and sophisticated understanding of my research area or topic?"
- "Can you suggest some ways to use primary sources to address and challenge existing assumptions and ideas in my research area or topic in [insert writing sample here]?"
- "How can I use primary sources to support my claims and arguments while avoiding plagiarism and maintaining academic integrity in [insert writing sample here]?"

Supporting arguments

- "Can you provide some suggestions on how to generate examples that support my argument in [insert writing sample here]?"
- "I'm struggling to find relevant and effective examples to support my argument in my paper on [research area or topic]. Can you provide some guidance?"
- "How can I use examples to strengthen my argument and make it more convincing in [insert writing sample here]?"
- "Can you suggest some ways to use real-life scenarios or case studies to support my argument in [insert writing sample here]?"
- "I need help identifying examples that are appropriate and relevant to my argument in [insert writing sample here]. Can you provide some guidance on how to find them?"
- "What strategies can I use to use examples to explain complex or abstract ideas in [insert writing sample here]?"
- "Can you suggest some effective ways to use anecdotes or personal experiences to support my argument in [insert writing sample here]?"
- "I'm having trouble finding specific examples to support my argument in my paper on [area of interest]. Can you provide some guidance on how to approach this?"
- "How can I use examples to address potential counterarguments or objections to my argument in [insert writing sample here]?"

- "Can you provide some suggestions on how to use statistics or data to support my argument in [insert writing sample here]?"
- "I need help finding relevant examples that are current and up-to-date in my research area or topic. Can you provide some guidance on how to do this?"
- "What strategies can I use to use examples to create a more engaging and interesting paper in [insert writing sample here]?"
- "Can you suggest some ways to use examples from different cultures or perspectives to support my argument in [insert writing sample here]?"
- "I'm struggling to find examples that are accessible and understandable for my intended audience in [insert writing sample here]. Can you provide some guidance?"
- "How can I use examples to show the practical application of my research findings in [insert writing sample here]?"

Supporting arguments

- "Can you provide some suggestions on how to use hypothetical scenarios or thought experiments to support my argument in [insert writing sample here]?"
- "I need help finding relevant examples that are credible and trustworthy in my research area or topic. Can you provide some guidance on how to evaluate them?"
- "What strategies can I use to use examples to create a more compelling and persuasive argument in [insert writing sample here]?"
- "Can you suggest some effective ways to use examples to make my argument more relatable and relevant to my intended audience in [insert writing sample here]?"
- "I'm having trouble finding examples that are unique and original in my research area or topic. Can you provide some guidance on how to approach this?"

Abstracts and summaries

- "Can you provide some guidance on how to write an effective abstract for [insert writing sample here] that accurately summarizes the key points and findings?"
- "I'm struggling to write a clear and concise summary of my research in [research area or topic]. Can you suggest some strategies for improving it?"
- "How can I effectively convey the purpose, scope, and significance of my research in an abstract or summary in [insert writing sample here]?"
- "Can you suggest some ways to use language and structure to create an engaging and informative summary of my research in [insert writing sample here]?"
- "I need help identifying the most important information to include in an abstract or summary of my research in [research area or topic]. Can you provide some guidance?"
- "What strategies can I use to tailor my abstract or summary to the intended audience and purpose of my research in [insert writing sample here]?"
- "Can you provide some suggestions on how to use keywords and phrases effectively in an abstract or summary of my research in [research area or topic]?"
- "I'm having trouble determining the appropriate length and level of detail for my abstract or summary in [insert writing sample here]. Can you provide some guidance on how to approach this?"

- "How can I use the abstract or summary to highlight the originality and contribution of my research in [insert writing sample here]?"
- "Can you suggest some effective ways to use the abstract or summary to establish the relevance and importance of my research in [insert writing sample here]?"
- "I need help structuring my abstract or summary to effectively convey the main points and findings of my research in [research area or topic]. Can you provide some guidance?"
- "What strategies can I use to effectively convey the methodology and approach of my research in an abstract or summary in [insert writing sample here]?"
- "Can you provide some suggestions on how to use the abstract or summary to convey the implications and significance of my research in [insert writing sample here]?"
- "I'm struggling to write an abstract or summary that accurately reflects the content and scope of my research in [research area or topic]. Can you suggest some strategies for improving it?"
- "How can I use the abstract or summary to engage the reader and generate interest in my research in [insert writing sample here]?"
- "Can you suggest some ways to use the abstract or summary to convey the contribution and impact of my research in [research area or topic]?"
- "I need help identifying the appropriate tone and style for my abstract or summary in [insert writing sample here]. Can you provide some guidance on how to approach this?"

Abstracts and summaries

- "What strategies can I use to effectively summarize the main arguments and findings of my research in an abstract or summary in [research area or topic]?"
- "Can you provide some suggestions on how to use the abstract or summary to situate my research within the broader context of the field in [insert writing sample here]?"
- "I'm having trouble writing an abstract or summary that effectively conveys the main purpose and findings of my research in [research area or topic]. Can you suggest some strategies for improving it?"

Tables and figures assistance

- "I'm having trouble formatting my tables and figures in [insert writing sample here]. Can you provide some guidance on how to effectively present my data?"
- "Can you suggest some ways to use formatting and design to make my tables and figures more visually appealing and informative in [insert writing sample here]?"
- "How can I use tables and figures to effectively present complex data and findings in [insert writing sample here]?"
- "Can you provide some guidance on how to label and caption my tables and figures in [insert writing sample here] to make them more understandable and informative?"
- "I need help identifying the most appropriate types of tables and figures to use for my data in [research area or topic]. Can you provide some guidance?"
- "What strategies can I use to effectively integrate my tables and figures with the rest of my text in [insert writing sample here]?"
- "Can you suggest some ways to use tables and figures to effectively convey trends and patterns in my data in [insert writing sample here]?"
- "I'm struggling to format my tables and figures in a way that is consistent and easy to follow in [insert writing sample here]. Can you provide some guidance on how to approach this?"

- "How can I use tables and figures to highlight the most important findings and results of my research in [insert writing sample here]?"
- "Can you provide some suggestions on how to use color and contrast effectively in my tables and figures to make them more visually engaging in [insert writing sample here]?"
- "I need help determining the appropriate size and resolution for my tables and figures in [insert writing sample here]. Can you provide some guidance on how to approach this?"
- "What strategies can I use to effectively annotate and explain my tables and figures in [insert writing sample here] to make them more informative and understandable?"
- "Can you suggest some ways to use tables and figures to support my argument and strengthen my claims in [insert writing sample here]?"
- "I'm struggling to fit my tables and figures within the page limits of my paper in [research area or topic]. Can you provide some guidance on how to approach this?"
- "How can I use tables and figures to effectively compare and contrast different aspects of my data and findings in [insert writing sample here]?"
- "Can you provide some suggestions on how to use tables and figures to effectively summarize my data and findings in [insert writing sample here]?"
- "I need help formatting my tables and figures in a way that is accessible and understandable for my intended audience in [insert writing sample here]. Can you provide some guidance?"

Tables and figures assistance

- "What strategies can I use to effectively present my qualitative data in tables and figures in [research area or topic]?"
- "Can you suggest some ways to use tables and figures to effectively present my quantitative data in [insert writing sample here]?"
- "I'm having trouble determining the appropriate amount of detail to include in my tables and figures in [insert writing sample here]. Can you provide some guidance on how to approach this?"

Discussion questions

- "Can you suggest some open-ended questions that would be appropriate for discussion of my research findings in [insert writing sample here]?"
- "I'm struggling to generate thought-provoking discussion questions based on my research in [research area or topic]. Can you provide some guidance on how to approach this?"
- "How can I use discussion questions to engage my audience and promote critical thinking about my research in [insert writing sample here]?"
- "Can you suggest some ways to use discussion questions to encourage participants to share their own experiences and insights related to my research in [insert writing sample here]?"
- "I need help generating discussion questions that are relevant and specific to my research area or topic. Can you provide some guidance on how to do this?"
- "What strategies can I use to generate discussion questions that foster collaboration and exchange of ideas among participants in [insert writing sample here]?"
- "Can you provide some suggestions on how to use discussion questions to encourage participants to consider different perspectives and interpretations of my research in [insert writing sample here]?"
- "I'm having trouble generating discussion questions that are appropriate for different levels of expertise and knowledge in [research area or topic]. Can you provide some guidance on how to approach this?"

- "How can I use discussion questions to elicit feedback and constructive criticism about my research in [insert writing sample here]?"
- "Can you suggest some ways to use discussion questions to explore the implications and applications of my research findings in [insert writing sample here]?"
- "I need help generating discussion questions that are focused and relevant to the specific objectives and research questions of my study in [research area or topic]. Can you provide some guidance on how to do this?"
- "What strategies can I use to generate discussion questions that are engaging and thought-provoking for participants in [insert writing sample here]?"
- "Can you provide some suggestions on how to use discussion questions to explore the potential limitations and future directions of my research in [insert writing sample here]?"
- "I'm struggling to generate discussion questions that are appropriate for different settings and contexts (e.g. classroom, conference, online discussion) in [research area or topic]. Can you provide some guidance on how to approach this?"
- "How can I use discussion questions to encourage participants to apply my research findings to their own experiences and practices in [insert writing sample here]?"

Discussion questions

- "Can you suggest some ways to use discussion questions to highlight the relevance and significance of my research in [research area or topic] for different audiences?"
- "I need help generating discussion questions that are innovative and thought-provoking in [research area or topic]. Can you provide some guidance on how to do this?"
- "What strategies can I use to generate discussion questions that are accessible and understandable for participants with different backgrounds and experiences in [insert writing sample here]?"
- "Can you provide some suggestions on how to use discussion questions to create a constructive and respectful environment for participants to share their perspectives and ideas in [insert writing sample here]?"
- "I'm having trouble generating discussion questions that are appropriate for the goals and objectives of my study in [research area or topic]. Can you provide some guidance on how to approach this?"

Supervisor feedback and revising your writing

- "I received feedback from my supervisor [insert supervisor feedback here] on [insert current writing sample here]. Can you provide some suggestions on how to incorporate this feedback effectively?"
- "How can I use feedback from my supervisor [insert supervisor feedback here] to improve the clarity and coherence of my writing in [insert current writing sample here]?"
- "Can you suggest some ways to revise my writing in [insert current writing sample here] to address the specific concerns and suggestions raised by my supervisor [insert supervisor feedback here]?"
- "I need help identifying the most important areas to focus on when revising my writing in response to feedback from my supervisor [insert supervisor feedback here]. Can you provide some guidance on how to do this?"
- "What strategies can I use to effectively incorporate the feedback from my supervisor [insert supervisor feedback here] while maintaining the integrity and coherence of my writing in [insert current writing sample here]?"
- "Can you suggest some ways to use feedback from my supervisor [insert supervisor feedback here] to strengthen the argument and evidence presented in my writing in [insert current writing sample here]?"

Supervisor feedback and revising your writing

- "I'm struggling to revise my writing in a way that reflects the feedback and suggestions provided by my supervisor [insert supervisor feedback here]. Can you provide some guidance on how to approach this?"
- "How can I use feedback from my supervisor [insert supervisor feedback here] to improve the organization and structure of my writing in [insert current writing sample here]?"
- "Can you suggest some ways to revise my writing in [insert current writing sample here] to more effectively address the research question and objectives, as suggested by my supervisor [insert supervisor feedback here]?"
- "I need help using feedback from my supervisor [insert supervisor feedback here] to improve the clarity and coherence of my writing style in [insert current writing sample here]. Can you provide some guidance on how to do this?"
- "What strategies can I use to effectively incorporate the feedback from my supervisor [insert supervisor feedback here] while maintaining the appropriate tone and style in my writing in [insert current writing sample here]?"
- "Can you suggest some ways to use feedback from my supervisor [insert supervisor feedback here] to more effectively address the potential limitations and implications of my research in [insert current writing sample here]?"

Supervisor feedback and revising your writing

- "I'm having trouble revising my writing in response to feedback from my supervisor [insert supervisor feedback here] while maintaining the coherence and flow of my argument in [insert current writing sample here]. Can you provide some guidance on how to approach this?"

- "How can I use feedback from my supervisor [insert supervisor feedback here] to improve the use of evidence and citation in my writing in [insert current writing sample here]?"

- "Can you suggest some ways to revise my writing in [insert current writing sample here] to more effectively integrate feedback from my supervisor [insert supervisor feedback here] with my own ideas and arguments?"

- "I need help identifying the appropriate level of detail and specificity to include in my writing in response to feedback from my supervisor [insert supervisor feedback here]. Can you provide some guidance on how to approach this?"

- "What strategies can I use to effectively incorporate the feedback from my supervisor [insert supervisor feedback here] while maintaining the appropriate level of objectivity and neutrality in my writing in [insert current writing sample here]?"

- "Can you suggest some ways to use feedback from my supervisor [insert supervisor feedback here] to more effectively situate my research within the broader context of the field in [insert current writing sample here]?"

- "I'm struggling to revise my writing in a way that addresses the feedback from my supervisor [insert supervisor feedback here] without sacrificing the coherence and consistency of my argument in [insert current writing sample here]. Can you provide some guidance on how to do this?"
- "How can I use feedback from my supervisor [insert supervisor feedback here] to improve the overall quality and impact of my writing in [insert current writing sample here]?"

Case studies or case-based papers

- "Can you suggest some specific examples or cases that would be appropriate for a case-based paper on [research area or topic]?"
- "I'm having trouble identifying specific cases or examples that would effectively illustrate the key concepts and theories in [research area or topic]. Can you provide some guidance on how to approach this?"
- "What strategies can I use to effectively select and analyze cases for a case study in [research area or topic]?"
- "Can you suggest some ways to use case studies to explore the practical applications and implications of my research in [research area or topic]?"
- "I need help identifying the most appropriate types of cases or examples to use for my case-based paper in [research area or topic]. Can you provide some guidance on how to approach this?"
- "How can I use case studies to effectively demonstrate the relevance and significance of my research in [research area or topic] for different stakeholders and audiences?"
- "Can you provide some suggestions on how to use case studies to highlight the diversity and complexity of experiences and perspectives related to my research in [research area or topic]?"

- "I'm struggling to identify specific cases or examples that would effectively illustrate the ethical considerations and dilemmas in [research area or topic]. Can you provide some guidance on how to approach this?"
- "What strategies can I use to effectively integrate quantitative and qualitative data in my case study analysis in [research area or topic]?"
- "Can you suggest some ways to use case studies to explore the historical and cultural contexts of my research in [research area or topic]?"
- "I need help generating research questions and hypotheses for my case-based paper in [research area or topic]. Can you provide some guidance on how to approach this?"
- "How can I use case studies to effectively analyze and interpret the impact and outcomes of my research in [research area or topic]?"
- "Can you provide some suggestions on how to use case studies to explore the role of different stakeholders and institutions in my research area or topic?"
- "I'm struggling to identify specific cases or examples that would effectively illustrate the theoretical frameworks and concepts in [research area or topic]. Can you provide some guidance on how to approach this?"
- "What strategies can I use to effectively use storytelling and narrative techniques in my case study analysis in [research area or topic]?"

Case studies or case-based papers

- "Can you suggest some ways to use case studies to explore the potential solutions and interventions for the issues and challenges in my research area or topic?"
- "I need help identifying the appropriate level of detail and specificity to include in my case study analysis in [research area or topic]. Can you provide some guidance on how to approach this?"
- "How can I use case studies to effectively explore the connections and intersections between different aspects of my research in [research area or topic]?"
- "Can you provide some suggestions on how to use case studies to identify gaps and opportunities for future research in [research area or topic]?"
- "I'm struggling to identify specific cases or examples that would effectively illustrate the social, cultural, and political implications of my research in [research area or topic]. Can you provide some guidance on how to approach this?"

Notes

71

Persuasive arguments

- "How can I develop a more persuasive argument in [insert writing sample here] that effectively addresses the research question or problem?"
- "What strategies can I use to effectively integrate evidence and examples in my writing to support my argument in [insert writing sample here]?"
- "Can you provide some suggestions on how to use persuasive language and rhetorical strategies to make my argument more compelling in [insert writing sample here]?"
- "I need help identifying the most persuasive and relevant counterarguments to address in my writing in [insert writing sample here]. Can you provide some guidance on how to approach this?"
- "What strategies can I use to effectively use analogies and metaphors to make my argument more accessible and engaging to different audiences in [insert writing sample here]?"
- "Can you suggest some ways to use storytelling and narrative techniques to make my argument more compelling and memorable in [insert writing sample here]?"
- "I'm struggling to identify the most convincing and reliable sources of evidence to support my argument in [insert writing sample here]. Can you provide some guidance on how to approach this?"
- "How can I use persuasive language and rhetoric to effectively appeal to the emotions and values of my readers in [insert writing sample here]?"

- "Can you provide some suggestions on how to use visual aids and multimedia tools to enhance the persuasive impact of my writing in [insert writing sample here]?"
- "I need help identifying the most important and relevant points to emphasize in my argument in [insert writing sample here]. Can you provide some guidance on how to approach this?"
- "What strategies can I use to effectively use humor and irony to make my argument more engaging and memorable in [insert writing sample here]?"
- "Can you suggest some ways to use examples and case studies to illustrate the practical and real-world implications of my argument in [insert writing sample here]?"
- "I'm struggling to effectively balance the use of evidence and rhetorical strategies in my writing to support my argument in [insert writing sample here]. Can you provide some guidance on how to approach this?"
- "How can I use persuasive language and rhetoric to effectively appeal to the reason and logic of my readers in [insert writing sample here]?"
- "Can you provide some suggestions on how to use the appropriate tone and style to effectively communicate my argument to different audiences in [insert writing sample here]?"
- "I need help identifying the most appropriate and effective means of presenting and organizing my evidence and examples in [insert writing sample here]. Can you provide some guidance on how to approach this?"

Persuasive arguments

- "What strategies can I use to effectively anticipate and address potential objections and counterarguments in my writing in [insert writing sample here]?"
- "Can you suggest some ways to use persuasive language and rhetoric to effectively appeal to the authority and expertise of my readers in [insert writing sample here]?"
- "I'm struggling to effectively use transitions and signposts to connect the different parts of my argument in [insert writing sample here]. Can you provide some guidance on how to approach this?"
- "How can I use persuasive language and rhetoric to effectively appeal to the values and beliefs of my readers in [insert writing sample here]?"

Evidence to support your arguments

- "What strategies can I use to effectively integrate evidence and examples in my writing to support my argument in [insert writing sample here]?"
- "I need help identifying the most persuasive and reliable sources of evidence to support my argument in [insert writing sample here]. Can you provide some guidance on how to approach this?"
- "Can you suggest some ways to use empirical data and research findings to support my argument in [insert writing sample here]?"
- "I'm struggling to effectively use the research literature to support my argument in [insert writing sample here]. Can you provide some guidance on how to approach this?"
- "What strategies can I use to effectively synthesize and integrate the relevant evidence and research findings to support my argument in [insert writing sample here]?"
- "Can you provide some suggestions on how to effectively evaluate and analyze the quality and relevance of the evidence used to support my argument in [insert writing sample here]?"
- "I need help identifying the most significant and relevant examples and case studies to use in my writing to support my argument in [insert writing sample here]. Can you provide some guidance on how to approach this?"

- "What strategies can I use to effectively use statistical data and trends to support my argument in [insert writing sample here]?"
- "Can you suggest some ways to use expert opinions and perspectives to support my argument in [insert writing sample here]?"
- "I'm struggling to effectively use direct quotes and paraphrases to support my argument in [insert writing sample here]. Can you provide some guidance on how to approach this?"
- "What strategies can I use to effectively use visuals and multimedia tools to enhance the presentation and impact of the evidence used to support my argument in [insert writing sample here]?"
- "Can you provide some suggestions on how to effectively use primary and secondary sources to support my argument in [insert writing sample here]?"
- "I need help identifying the most appropriate and effective means of presenting and organizing the evidence used to support my argument in [insert writing sample here]. Can you provide some guidance on how to approach this?"
- "What strategies can I use to effectively anticipate and address potential criticisms and counterarguments to the evidence used to support my argument in [insert writing sample here]?"
- "Can you suggest some ways to use examples and analogies to make the evidence used to support my argument in [insert writing sample here] more accessible and engaging to different audiences?"

Evidence to support your arguments

- "I'm struggling to effectively use the relevant laws, policies, and regulations to support my argument in [insert writing sample here]. Can you provide some guidance on how to approach this?"
- "What strategies can I use to effectively use historical and cultural references to support my argument in [insert writing sample here]?"
- "Can you provide some suggestions on how to effectively use anecdotal evidence and personal experiences to support my argument in [insert writing sample here]?"
- "I need help identifying the most appropriate and effective means of citing and referencing the evidence used to support my argument in [insert writing sample here]. Can you provide some guidance on how to approach this?"
- "What strategies can I use to effectively use the evidence to draw meaningful and relevant conclusions that support my argument in [insert writing sample here]?"

Reflective essays or personal statements

- "Can you suggest some ways to effectively communicate my personal and professional experiences and growth in [insert research area or topic] through my reflective essay or personal statement?"
- "I'm struggling to identify the most significant and relevant experiences and achievements to include in my reflective essay or personal statement. Can you provide some guidance on how to approach this?"
- "What strategies can I use to effectively use the reflective essay or personal statement to demonstrate my potential contributions and goals in [insert research area or topic]?"
- "Can you provide some suggestions on how to use storytelling and narrative techniques to make my reflective essay or personal statement more engaging and memorable?"
- "I need help identifying the most appropriate and effective means of communicating my values and motivations in my reflective essay or personal statement. Can you provide some guidance on how to approach this?"
- "What strategies can I use to effectively use the reflective essay or personal statement to demonstrate my unique perspective and potential in [insert research area or topic]?"

Reflective essays or personal statements

- "Can you suggest some ways to use examples and evidence to support the claims and assertions made in my reflective essay or personal statement?"
- "I'm struggling to effectively use the reflective essay or personal statement to showcase my relevant skills and experiences in [insert research area or topic]. Can you provide some guidance on how to approach this?"
- "What strategies can I use to effectively use the reflective essay or personal statement to demonstrate my potential to contribute to research and scholarship in [insert research area or topic]?"
- "Can you provide some suggestions on how to effectively use the reflective essay or personal statement to showcase my passion and enthusiasm for [insert research area or topic]?"
- "I need help identifying the most appropriate and effective means of organizing and structuring my reflective essay or personal statement. Can you provide some guidance on how to approach this?"
- "What strategies can I use to effectively use the reflective essay or personal statement to showcase my potential to collaborate and communicate with others in [insert research area or topic]?"
- "Can you suggest some ways to use the reflective essay or personal statement to showcase my potential to adapt and thrive in challenging situations or environments in [insert research area or topic]?"

Reflective essays or personal statements

- "I'm struggling to effectively use the reflective essay or personal statement to demonstrate my potential to make a meaningful and significant impact in [insert research area or topic]. Can you provide some guidance on how to approach this?"
- "What strategies can I use to effectively use the reflective essay or personal statement to demonstrate my potential to innovate and explore new ideas and approaches in [insert research area or topic]?"
- "Can you provide some suggestions on how to use the reflective essay or personal statement to showcase my potential to connect my research or scholarship to real-world issues and challenges in [insert research area or topic]?"
- "I need help identifying the most effective and persuasive language and rhetoric to use in my reflective essay or personal statement. Can you provide some guidance on how to approach this?"
- "What strategies can I use to effectively use the reflective essay or personal statement to demonstrate my potential to contribute to diversity, equity, and inclusion in [insert research area or topic]?"
- "Can you suggest some ways to use the reflective essay or personal statement to showcase my potential to make a positive and lasting impact on my community or society in [insert research area or topic]?"
- "I'm struggling to effectively use the reflective essay or personal statement to demonstrate my potential to grow and develop as a researcher or scholar in [insert research area or topic]. Can you provide some guidance on how to approach this?"

Rhetorical devices

- "What are some effective ways to use repetition and parallelism to enhance the impact of my argument in [insert writing sample here]?"
- "I need help identifying the most appropriate and effective rhetorical devices to use in my writing to achieve my intended purpose and audience. Can you provide some guidance on how to approach this?"
- "Can you suggest some ways to use rhetorical questions and analogies to make my writing more engaging and persuasive in [insert writing sample here]?"
- "I'm struggling to effectively use the rhetorical device of pathos to emotionally connect with my audience in [insert writing sample here]. Can you provide some guidance on how to approach this?"
- "What strategies can I use to effectively use the rhetorical device of logos to logically persuade my audience in [insert writing sample here]?"
- "Can you provide some suggestions on how to use the rhetorical device of ethos to establish my credibility and authority in [insert writing sample here]?"
- "I need help identifying the most effective and persuasive language and rhetoric to use in my writing to achieve my intended purpose and audience. Can you provide some guidance on how to approach this?"
- "What strategies can I use to effectively use the rhetorical device of hyperbole to emphasize the importance and impact of my argument in [insert writing sample here]?"

- "Can you suggest some ways to use the rhetorical device of allusion to make my writing more memorable and impactful in [insert writing sample here]?"
- "I'm struggling to effectively use the rhetorical device of irony to create a sense of humor or satire in my writing in [insert writing sample here]. Can you provide some guidance on how to approach this?"
- "What strategies can I use to effectively use the rhetorical device of antithesis to create a sense of contrast and balance in my writing in [insert writing sample here]?"
- "Can you provide some suggestions on how to use the rhetorical device of euphemism to make my writing more polite or tactful in [insert writing sample here]?"
- "I need help identifying the most effective and persuasive ways to use the rhetorical device of analogy to explain complex or abstract concepts in [insert writing sample here]. Can you provide some guidance on how to approach this?"
- "What strategies can I use to effectively use the rhetorical device of personification to make my writing more vivid and engaging in [insert writing sample here]?"
- "Can you suggest some ways to use the rhetorical device of onomatopoeia to create a sense of sound or rhythm in my writing in [insert writing sample here]?"
- "I'm struggling to effectively use the rhetorical device of metonymy to refer to something using a related term or concept in my writing in [insert writing sample here]. Can you provide some guidance on how to approach this?"

Rhetorical devices

- "What strategies can I use to effectively use the rhetorical device of synecdoche to refer to a part of something to represent the whole in my writing in [insert writing sample here]?"
- "Can you provide some suggestions on how to use the rhetorical device of understatement to create a sense of modesty or sarcasm in my writing in [insert writing sample here]?"
- "I need help identifying the most effective and persuasive ways to use the rhetorical device of chiasmus to create a sense of symmetry and balance in my writing in [insert writing sample here]. Can you provide some guidance on how to approach this?"
- "What strategies can I use to effectively use the rhetorical device of juxtaposition to create a sense of contrast and comparison in my writing in [insert writing sample here]?"

Developing a strong argument

- "Can you provide feedback on the strength of my main argument in [insert writing sample here]? What suggestions do you have for improving its persuasiveness?"
- "I'm struggling to effectively counter potential objections and alternative perspectives in my argument in [insert writing sample here]. Can you provide some guidance on how to approach this?"
- "What strategies can I use to effectively use evidence and examples to support and strengthen my argument in [insert writing sample here]?"
- "Can you suggest some ways to anticipate and address potential counterarguments and critiques in my argument in [insert writing sample here]?"
- "I'm having trouble identifying the most effective and persuasive ways to structure and organize my argument in [insert writing sample here]. Can you provide some guidance on how to approach this?"
- "What strategies can I use to effectively use rhetorical devices and persuasive language to strengthen my argument in [insert writing sample here]?"
- "Can you provide some suggestions on how to use logical fallacies and biases to avoid weakening my argument in [insert writing sample here]?"
- "I need help identifying the most appropriate and effective sources of evidence and examples to use in my argument in [insert writing sample here]. Can you provide some guidance on how to approach this?"

- "What strategies can I use to effectively use data and statistics to support and strengthen my argument in [insert writing sample here]?"
- "Can you suggest some ways to use real-world examples and case studies to make my argument more tangible and relevant in [insert writing sample here]?"
- "I'm struggling to effectively use theoretical concepts and frameworks to support my argument in [insert writing sample here]. Can you provide some guidance on how to approach this?"
- "What strategies can I use to effectively use historical evidence and context to strengthen my argument in [insert writing sample here]?"
- "Can you provide some suggestions on how to use anecdotal evidence and personal experiences to make my argument more relatable and compelling in [insert writing sample here]?"
- "I need help identifying the most effective and persuasive ways to use language and tone to convey my argument in [insert writing sample here]. Can you provide some guidance on how to approach this?"
- "What strategies can I use to effectively use analogies and metaphors to clarify and enhance my argument in [insert writing sample here]?"
- "Can you suggest some ways to use the opinions and perspectives of experts and authorities to support and strengthen my argument in [insert writing sample here]?"

Developing a strong argument

- "I'm struggling to effectively use the perspectives and experiences of marginalized or underrepresented groups to strengthen my argument in [insert writing sample here]. Can you provide some guidance on how to approach this?"
- "What strategies can I use to effectively use the perspectives and experiences of diverse groups to support and strengthen my argument in [insert writing sample here]?"
- "Can you provide some suggestions on how to use the rhetorical device of framing to shape how my argument is perceived and understood in [insert writing sample here]?"
- "I need help identifying the most effective and persuasive ways to use emotion and empathy to connect with my audience and enhance my argument in [insert writing sample here]. Can you provide some guidance on how to approach this?"

Shorten your text

- "How can I condense [insert writing sample here] without losing any essential information or clarity?"
- "What are some ways to simplify this paragraph on [specific methodology or approach] in [research area] while still accurately conveying its meaning in a shorter format?"
- "How can I shorten this sentence on [specific finding or result] in [research area] without sacrificing its significance or accuracy?"
- "What are some strategies for summarizing this section on [specific theory or model] in [research area] without oversimplifying it?"
- "What are some ways to streamline this description of [specific dataset or sample] in [research area] without omitting any important details or sacrificing its accuracy?"
- "How can I shorten this sentence on [specific trend or pattern] in [research area] without sacrificing its clarity or precision?"
- "What are some techniques for making this section on [specific limitation or challenge] in [research area] more succinct while still conveying its complexity?"
- "What are some ways to condense this overview of [specific subfield or area] in [research area] without losing any important context or nuance?"
- "How can I rephrase this conclusion on [specific implication or application] in [research area] to make it more concise while still conveying its significance?"

- "What are some strategies for summarizing this literature review on [specific topic or phenomenon] in [research area] without overlooking any significant studies or perspectives?"
- "How can I make this discussion of [specific methodology or approach] in [research area] more concise without sacrificing its comprehensiveness or rigor?"
- "What are some techniques for simplifying this introduction to [specific research question or hypothesis] in [research area] without sacrificing its significance or novelty?"
- "How can I condense this paragraph on [specific theoretical framework or concept] in [research area] to make it more accessible to readers without diluting its intellectual depth or complexity?"
- "What are some ways to streamline this summary of [specific experiment or study] in [research area] without losing any important details or conclusions?"
- "How can I make this abstract on [specific research project or paper] in [research area] more concise and engaging without omitting any key information or takeaways?"
- "What are some techniques for simplifying this discussion of [specific variable or factor] in [research area] to make it more understandable to a broader audience without losing its significance?"
- "How can I shorten this section on [specific application or use case] of research in [research area] without sacrificing its real-world relevance or impact?"

Shorten your text

- "What are some ways to condense this section on [specific trend or development] in [research area] without overlooking any important context or nuances?"
- "How can I rephrase this sentence on [specific methodology or approach] in [research area] to make it more concise and actionable for readers?"
- "What are some techniques for simplifying this discussion of [specific challenge or obstacle] facing researchers in [research area] without losing any important details or considerations?"

Expand your text

- "How can I expand [insert writing sample here] to include additional information or insights that would enrich the reader's understanding of [specific topic or phenomenon] in [research area]?"
- "What are some ways to provide more context or background information in [insert writing sample here] to help readers better understand [specific aspect or feature] in [research area]?"
- "How can I add more examples or case studies to [insert writing sample here] to illustrate the relevance or significance of [specific finding or result] in [research area]?"
- "What are some strategies for elaborating on the limitations or challenges discussed in [insert writing sample here] and providing potential solutions or avenues for future research in [research area]?"
- "How can I include more discussion on the theoretical frameworks or conceptual models that underpin [insert writing sample here] in [research area] to help readers better understand its theoretical contributions?"
- "What are some ways to incorporate more empirical evidence or data analysis in [insert writing sample here] to support its claims and bolster its credibility in [research area]?"
- "How can I provide more detailed explanations of the methodology or approach used in [insert writing sample here] to help readers better understand its rigor and validity in [research area]?"

- "What are some strategies for incorporating more perspectives or voices from relevant stakeholders or experts in [insert writing sample here] to enrich its analysis and provide diverse viewpoints in [research area]?"
- "How can I expand on the practical implications or applications of [insert writing sample here] in [research area] to help readers understand its relevance to real-world issues or challenges?"
- "What are some ways to include more discussion on the historical or cultural context surrounding [insert writing sample here] to help readers understand its significance and relevance in [research area]?"
- "How can I provide more detailed analysis or interpretation of the results presented in [insert writing sample here] to help readers better understand the significance of the findings in [research area]?"
- "What are some strategies for incorporating more discussion on the ethical or social implications of [insert writing sample here] in [research area] to help readers understand its broader implications for society and individuals?"
- "How can I expand on the literature review presented in [insert writing sample here] to include more relevant studies or theories in [research area] and provide a more comprehensive overview of the field?"
- "What are some ways to incorporate more discussion on the practical challenges or considerations involved in conducting research on [specific topic or phenomenon] in [research area] to help readers understand its complexities and nuances?"

Expand your text

- "How can I include more discussion on the methodology or approach used in [insert writing sample here] to highlight its strengths and weaknesses in [research area] and provide a more nuanced evaluation of its efficacy?"
- "What are some strategies for incorporating more discussion on the policy implications of [insert writing sample here] in [research area] to help readers understand its relevance to policymakers and decision-makers?"
- "How can I expand on the discussion of the results presented in [insert writing sample here] to include more detailed analysis or sub-analyses in [research area] and provide a more granular understanding of the findings?"
- "What are some ways to include more discussion on the theoretical debates or controversies surrounding [insert writing sample here] in [research area] to help readers understand its place in the broader academic discourse?"
- "How can I provide more detailed explanations or illustrations of the key concepts or terms used in [insert writing sample here] to help readers better understand the terminology and its relevance in [research area]?"
- "What are some strategies for expanding on the discussion of the limitations or challenges faced in [insert writing sample here] to provide a more detailed analysis of their implications for future research and practice in [research area]?"

Notes

Clarity

- "How can I rephrase this sentence on [specific finding or result] in [research area] to make it more concise and impactful? [insert writing sample here]"
- "What are some ways to simplify this paragraph on [specific methodology or approach] in [research area] while still accurately conveying its meaning? [insert writing sample here]"
- "What are some strategies for summarizing this section on [specific theory or model] in [research area] without oversimplifying it? [insert writing sample here]"
- "What are some ways to streamline this description of [specific dataset or sample] in [research area] without omitting any important details? [insert writing sample here]"
- "What are some techniques for making this section on [specific limitation or challenge] in [research area] more succinct while still conveying its complexity?"
- "What are some ways to condense this overview of [specific subfield or area] in [research area] without losing any important context or nuance? [insert writing sample here]"
- "How can I rephrase this conclusion on [specific implication or application] in [research area] to make it more concise and memorable? [insert writing sample here]"
- "What are some strategies for summarizing this literature review on [specific topic or phenomenon] in [research area] without overlooking any significant studies or perspectives? [insert writing sample here]"

- "How can I make this discussion of [specific methodology or approach] in [research area] more concise without sacrificing its comprehensiveness or rigor? [insert writing sample here]"
- "What are some techniques for simplifying this introduction to [specific research question or hypothesis] in [research area] without oversimplifying its significance or novelty? [insert writing sample here]"
- "How can I condense this paragraph on [specific theoretical framework or concept] in [research area] to make it more accessible to readers without diluting its intellectual depth or complexity? [insert writing sample here]"
- "What are some ways to streamline this summary of [specific experiment or study] in [research area] without losing any important details or conclusions? [insert writing sample here]"
- "How can I make this abstract on [specific research project or paper] in [research area] more concise and engaging without omitting any key information or takeaways? [insert writing sample here]"
- "What are some techniques for simplifying this discussion of [specific variable or factor] in [research area] to make it more understandable to a broader audience? [insert writing sample here]"
- "What are some ways to condense this section on [specific trend or development] in [research area] without overlooking any important context or nuances? [insert writing sample here]"

Clarity

- "How can I rephrase this sentence on [specific methodology or approach] in [research area] to make it more concise and actionable for readers? [insert writing sample here]"
- "What are some techniques for simplifying this discussion of [specific challenge or obstacle] facing researchers in [research area] without losing any important details or considerations? [insert writing sample here]"

Impact

- "How can I rephrase [insert writing sample here] to make it more impactful and memorable for readers in [research area]?"
- "What are some ways to add more vivid language or sensory details to [insert writing sample here] to make it more engaging and compelling for readers?"
- "How can I use metaphors or analogies to make [insert writing sample here] more accessible and understandable to readers in [research area]?"
- "What are some techniques for using anecdotes or personal stories to add emotional resonance to [insert writing sample here] in [research area]?"
- "How can I use statistics or data visualizations to make [insert writing sample here] more persuasive and impactful for readers in [research area]?"
- "What are some strategies for using rhetorical questions or vivid language to create a sense of urgency in [insert writing sample here] about [specific issue or problem] in [research area]?"
- "How can I use vivid language and sensory details to create a strong sense of place or atmosphere in [insert writing sample here] about [specific topic or phenomenon] in [research area]?"
- "What are some ways to use analogies or examples to illustrate complex concepts or theories in [insert writing sample here] about [specific aspect or feature] in [research area]?"

- "How can I use active verbs and concrete nouns to create a sense of momentum and energy in [insert writing sample here] about [specific finding or result] in [research area]?"
- "What are some techniques for using humor or irony to make [insert writing sample here] more engaging and memorable for readers in [research area]?"
- "How can I use sensory details and evocative language to create a strong emotional impact in [insert writing sample here] about [specific issue or problem] in [research area]?"
- "What are some strategies for using clear and concise language to communicate complex ideas in [insert writing sample here] about [specific theory or model] in [research area]?"
- "How can I use bold or provocative language to challenge readers' assumptions or beliefs in [insert writing sample here] about [specific topic or phenomenon] in [research area]?"
- "What are some ways to use quotes or testimonials from experts or stakeholders to add credibility and impact to [insert writing sample here] in [research area]?"
- "How can I use parallelism or repetition to create a sense of rhythm and momentum in [insert writing sample here] about [specific aspect or feature] in [research area]?"
- "What are some techniques for using suspense or surprise to create a sense of anticipation and engagement in [insert writing sample here] about [specific finding or result] in [research area]?"

Impact

- "How can I use vivid language and sensory details to create a sense of empathy and connection with readers in [insert writing sample here] about [specific population or group] in [research area]?"
- "What are some strategies for using clear and concise language to summarize complex data or information in [insert writing sample here] about [specific dataset or sample] in [research area]?"
- "How can I use rhetorical questions or vivid language to challenge readers' assumptions and stimulate critical thinking in [insert writing sample here] about [specific topic or issue] in [research area]?"
- "What are some ways to use vivid language and sensory details to create a sense of place and atmosphere in [insert writing sample here] about [specific area or region] in [research area]?"

Research methods ideas

- "In the context of [research area], what are some effective [research methods, e.g., qualitative, quantitative, or mixed methods] that could be employed to investigate [specific research question or hypothesis] and generate meaningful insights?"
- "Considering the unique challenges and complexities of studying [specific topic or phenomenon] in [research area], how can a researcher adapt or combine existing [research methods] to develop a more robust and comprehensive investigation approach?"
- "For a research project in [research area] that aims to explore [specific issue or question], what are some innovative data collection techniques or tools that can be used in conjunction with [research method] to enhance the quality and depth of the findings?"
- "How can a research project in [research area] effectively employ [research method] to investigate [specific topic or phenomenon] while ensuring the ethical considerations and the principles of responsible research are maintained?"
- "What are some successful examples or case studies of research projects in [research area] that have utilized [research method] to investigate [specific issue or challenge], and how can these be adapted or built upon for a new study?"

- "In the context of [research area], how can a researcher address potential biases, limitations, or confounding factors when using [research method] to investigate [specific research question or hypothesis], ensuring the validity and reliability of the findings?"
- "How can a research project in [research area] benefit from incorporating [research method] in a multi-method or interdisciplinary approach to explore [specific topic or phenomenon] and generate a more comprehensive understanding of the subject matter?"

Ethics applications

- "In the context of [research area], what are the key ethical considerations that should be addressed when conducting a research project involving [specific population or research subject], and how can these concerns be mitigated or managed effectively?"
- "How can a researcher ensure that the principles of informed consent, voluntary participation, and confidentiality are upheld throughout a research project in [research area], particularly when working with [specific population or data source]?"
- "When conducting research in [research area] that involves [specific vulnerable population or sensitive topic], what are some best practices for minimizing potential harm or distress to the participants, and how can these be implemented effectively?"
- "Considering the potential implications of a research project in [research area] on [specific stakeholder or community], how can a researcher actively engage these stakeholders in the research process to ensure that their perspectives and interests are considered and respected?"
- "In the context of [research area], how can a researcher ensure that data collection, storage, and analysis processes adhere to relevant ethical guidelines, legal requirements, and data protection regulations, particularly when working with [specific data source or sensitive information]?"

- "What are the potential conflicts of interest that may arise in a research project in [research area], particularly when working with [specific funding source, collaborator, or stakeholder], and how can these conflicts be identified, disclosed, and managed to maintain the integrity of the research?"
- "How can a researcher ensure that the dissemination and reporting of research findings in [research area] are conducted in a transparent, accurate, and unbiased manner, particularly when addressing [specific controversial issue or sensitive topic]?"

Bonus!

To unlock additional bonus material,
visit www.broneager.com/academic-phrasebook

For more great resources for writing with AI visit

BronEager.com

Hello

Thanks for buying, borrowing, finding (or perhaps stealing) this book! I created it to help researchers and academic writers benefit from the capabilities of AI.

If I haven't met you before, my *formal author bio* reads something like this:

Dr Bronwyn (Bron) Eager has an international reputation as a Scholarly Practitioner, with multi-disciplinary research interests spanning digital skills development, entrepreneurship, and the scholarship of teaching and learning. She has made contributions to the field of Artificial Intelligence (AI) through her work in developing training programs and offering guidance on enhancing digital literacies in higher education. She holds a PhD, Master of Entrepreneurship and Innovation (MEI) and a Graduate Certificate in Teaching and Learning (Higher Education).

But, a more authentic bio is this:

I'm passionate about digital tech and discovering how it can be used to enhance our lives. I get a lot of joy from sharing what I'm learning with others. I'm not an expert, just someone with boundless curiosity and the privilege to be able to spend time exploring.

I hope you enjoyed the book!

Bron
Visit BronEager.com to connect.

– The End –

Yet, just the beginning of your
AI-augmented research and
writing adventures!

As you go through your journey,
don't forget to prioritize taking
care of yourself.

For information on how to use AI
tools mindfully and maintain your
well-being in a society that
values excessive productivity,
check out:

CometWriter.com

Made in United States
Orlando, FL
14 September 2024